JOHN DEERE

BIG BOOK OF TRACTORS

Heather Alexander

DK Publishing

LONDON, NEW YORK, MUNICH,
MELBOURNE, and DELHI

Editor Nancy Ellwood
Senior Editor Elizabeth Hester
Designer Jessica Park
Managing Art Editor Michelle Baxter

Book Designer Annemarie Redmond

Special thanks to Daniel L. Dufner, John Deere
Waterloo Works, and Walter Ballauer

Published in the United States by
DK Publishing
375 Hudson Street
New York, NY 10014

07 08 09 10 11 10 9 8 7 6 5 4 3 2 1

Created and produced by
Parachute Publishing, L.L.C.
322 Eighth Avenue
New York, NY 10001

A catalog record for this book is
available from the Library of Congress.

ISBN-13: 978-0-7566-3213-7
ISBN-10: 0-7566-3213-7

Printed in China

Discover more at
www.dk.com

Contents

Tractors, tractors, tractors

The sun is rising to start a new day. Listen closely. *Vroom! Vroom!* Do you hear that? It's the sound of a tractor revving up, ready to begin working. Tractors are the most important machines on the farm because they make hard jobs a lot easier to do. There are many different kinds of tractors. They come in different shapes and sizes, and with different amounts of power. Tractors can do all kinds of jobs.

Spraying

Planting

Crawling

Clearing snow

Moving firewood

Baling hay

Harvesting

Meet John Deere

John Deere is the name of a big company that makes machines and equipment that do all kinds of jobs. They plow fields, plant and harvest crops, work at construction sites, and mow lawns. If you see a green and yellow tractor, you know that it's a John Deere tractor.

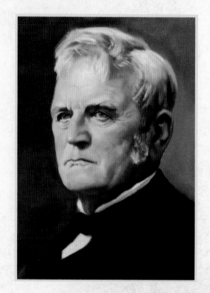

Who was John Deere?

John Deere was born in Vermont in 1804. As a teenager, he became a blacksmith. A blacksmith is someone who makes, or forges, things out of iron—shovels, shoes for horses, and wheels for wagons. John Deere became known for this and for creating new and better tools. In 1836, he moved to Illinois. Soon he would become famous for changing the world of farming.

Stuck in the mud

Many farmers like John Deere moved from the east to Illinois in search of new opportunities. But they weren't prepared for the rich, heavy soil they found there. Farmers had to stop often to clean the sticky soil off their plows. John Deere set out to make a new plow that would clean itself.

The first John Deere plow

John Deere made a plow with a smooth, steel blade. Steel could be polished so the sticky soil would slide off. He also curved the blade, which made the

plow cut through the soil better. He attached this new blade to wood handles and a beam that could be hooked onto horses, and it worked!

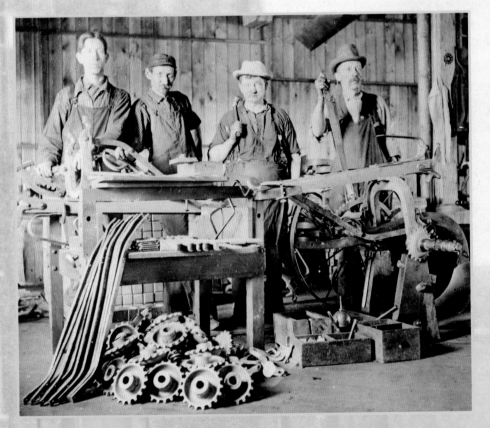

A winning combination

John Deere's first plow was a huge success. By 1842, he was selling 100 plows a year. In 1845, he built a factory and started his plow company. Then he had a new idea: make a lot of plows before he even got orders for them. For the first time, farmers could buy and use a plow right away.

The company grew and grew. Today, John Deere has about 47,000 employees worldwide, in 160 countries.

John Deere once said, "I will never put my name on a product that doesn't have in it the best that is in me." The company still holds this belief today, making the best machines possible.

A closer look

Let's take a closer look at a big tractor. This tractor is made up of more than 17,000 different parts. Here are some of the parts that you can see from the outside.

J.T.'s TRACTOR TRIVIA

The first tractors had only a steering wheel on their dashboard. Also there was no ignition key to start the tractor—the farmer had to turn a crank on the front of the tractor or spin a wheel on the side to get the engine going.

The exhaust pipe moves heat and burned gases away from the engine to keep the tractor safe.

The cab is where the driver sits.

Headlights are used when driving before sunrise, at night, or in bad weather.

Smaller front wheels work to turn the tractor.

Rearview and side mirrors allow the driver to see behind the tractor and on either side.

Large glass doors on both sides of the tractor make it easy for the driver to see the fields on either side.

Turn signals are lights that let other vehicles know when the tractor is about to turn.

The cab is high above the ground. Tractors have steps so the driver can climb into the cab.

Big rear wheels help the tractor ride over bumpy or muddy ground.

What is the Power Take-Off?

The engine gives the tractor power to go. But it can also share its power to make other machines go, too. The Power Take-Off System (PTO) is a metal pole on the back of the tractor. Important attachments called implements, such as plows and seed drills, are connected to the pole. When the engine is on, the power goes right through the PTO and into the implement to make it work.

The engine

Tractors are very big and heavy machines. They need a lot of power for all of the important jobs they do. The engine is the heart of the machine. It gives the tractor its power and makes the machine go.

Under the hood

Open the hood at the front of the tractor, and you'll find the tractor's engine. Inside the engine, fuel is burned in parts called cylinders. The more cylinders an engine has, the more powerful it is. This engine has six cylinders.

J.T.'s TRACTOR TRIVIA

Before the tractor was invented, the work on a farm stopped when the horses grew tired or hungry. A farmer would have to use about five acres of his land to grow food just for his horses. A tractor never gets tired, and it doesn't need to eat the crops. With fuel in its fuel tank, it can work all day and all night.

The valves let air and fuel into and out of the cylinder.

This is the connecting rod. It connects the piston to the crankshaft.

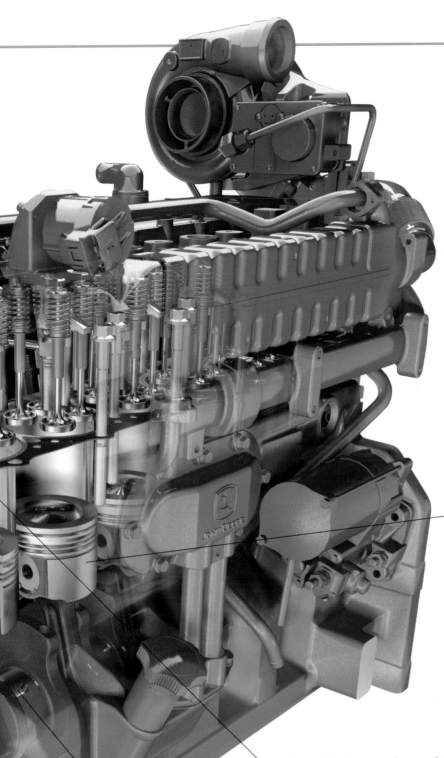

Horsepower

Before there were tractors, horses pulled plows on farms. Sometimes many horses were hitched together to give a farmer more "horsepower" for big jobs. Today, engine power is still called horsepower. So if a tractor has 250 horsepower, that means it can pull as much as 250 horses can.

The pistons move up and down when fuel is burned in the cylinder.

The cylinder is shaped like a tennis ball can. Inside the cylinder is the piston.

The moving pistons turn a rod, called the crankshaft, which gives power to the tractor.

Fill it up!

The fuel tank holds the gasoline that gives the engine power. The biggest tractor's tank can hold up to 300 gallons of fuel.

Inside the cab

The cab is where the driver sits. The cab is up high, so the driver can see the land all around, and it is enclosed to protect the driver from dust, severe weather, and the noise of the engine.

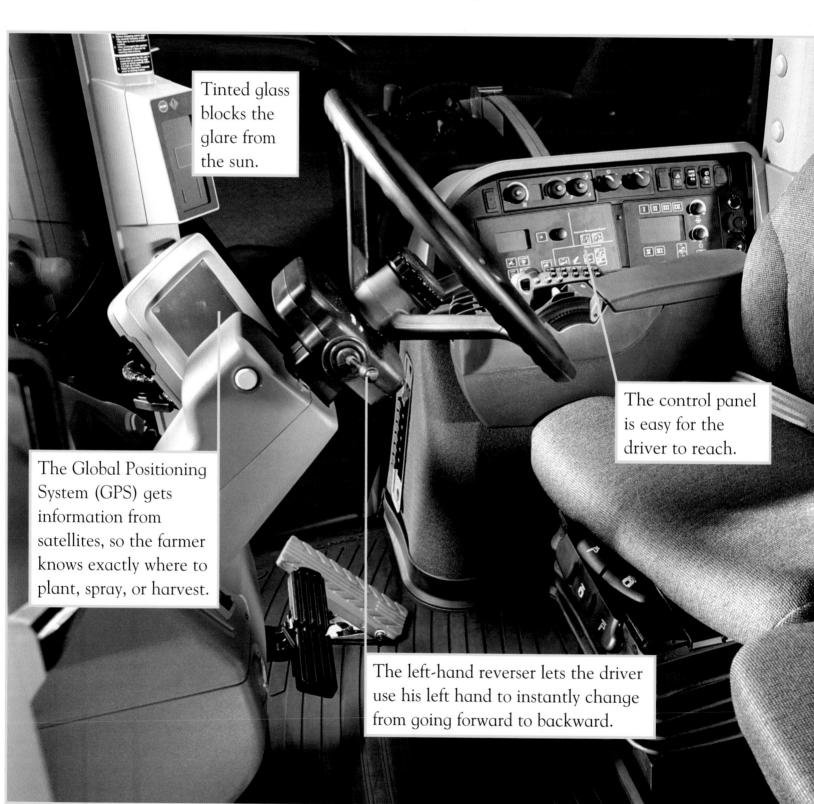

Tinted glass blocks the glare from the sun.

The control panel is easy for the driver to reach.

The Global Positioning System (GPS) gets information from satellites, so the farmer knows exactly where to plant, spray, or harvest.

The left-hand reverser lets the driver use his left hand to instantly change from going forward to backward.

Control panel

The control panel allows the driver to know everything that is going on as the tractor does its many jobs. That's why the tractor's brightly lit control panel is filled with knobs, buttons, gauges, dials, and joysticks.

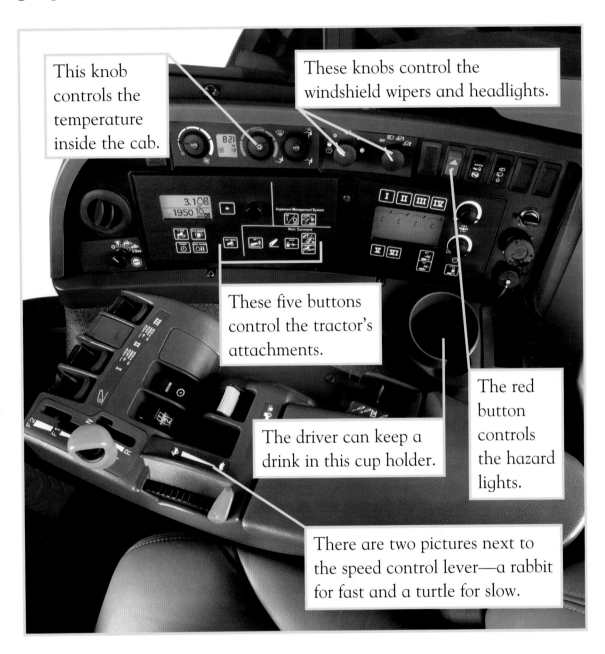

This knob controls the temperature inside the cab.

These knobs control the windshield wipers and headlights.

These five buttons control the tractor's attachments.

The red button controls the hazard lights.

The driver can keep a drink in this cup holder.

There are two pictures next to the speed control lever—a rabbit for fast and a turtle for slow.

The driver's seat is comfortably padded, since farmers often spend many hours sitting in the tractor.

J.T.'s TRACTOR TRIVIA

The engines of the first tractors were very loud and hurt farmers' ears. Now the farmer can sit in a quiet, soundproof cab and listen to music instead.

Wheels, tires, and tracks

Some tractors have wheels with tires. Other tractors have crawler tracks. Both allow heavy tractors to get a good grip on the ground as they do their tough work.

Round wheels

Most tractors have huge round wheels with rubber tires around them. The heavier a tractor is, the bigger the wheels and tires it needs in order to move.

The big fenders that cover the top of the rear wheels are called elephant ears. Fenders keep dirt from flying up toward the cab.

J.T.'s TRACTOR TRIVIA

When you want to turn a tractor with round wheels, you turn the steering wheel and both front tires turn. But a tractor with crawler tracks works differently. To turn a tractor with crawler tracks, only one set of the crawler tracks needs to move—the other side stays completely still. To turn left, for instance, the driver moves the right tracks and keeps the left side still.

The axle attaches the wheels to the tractor. The front axle turns the two front wheels together.

The long crawler tracks are especially good for muddy, snowy, or hilly areas.

Wheel rims are in the center of the wheels. You can spot John Deere tractors by the bright yellow wheel rims.

JOHN DEERE

8430T

Crawler tracks

Crawler tracks are huge steel belts that move around and around to make the tractor go forward or backward. They look like the treads you see on a bulldozer. With these tracks, the weight of the heavy tractor is spread out evenly, which keeps the tractor from sinking into soft or muddy land.

Into the groove

All tires have treads, which are grooves in the rubber. The treads help the tires grip the ground as the machine moves. This is called traction. Tractors often have deep treads, called lugs, to make sure the tractor never gets stuck in the mud. Lugs can be several inches deep.

Pick a pattern

Tractor tires come with many different tread patterns.

J.T.'s TRACTOR TRIVIA
The very first tractors didn't have tires. They just had metal wheels. Can you imagine how noisy and bumpy it would be driving metal wheels on pavement?

Agricultural tires have treads in diagonal lines. This keeps soil from sticking to the tires and gives excellent traction in muddy fields. But these tires are not good for lawns because they would damage the grass.

Turf tires have very shallow treads so they don't hurt grass or turf. They are usually found on lawn tractors, but are also good on roads.

Can you see the two different kinds of treads on the tires of this tractor and wagon?

Combination tires, also called industrial tires, have lugs that are wider and shallower than agricultural treads. They get good traction and are also good on turf. This tread was first used for construction tractors.

Front rib tires are used on the front wheels of smaller tractors, and are good in the dirt or on roads.

Inside out

Now that you've seen the parts of the tractor one by one, here's how they all fit together.

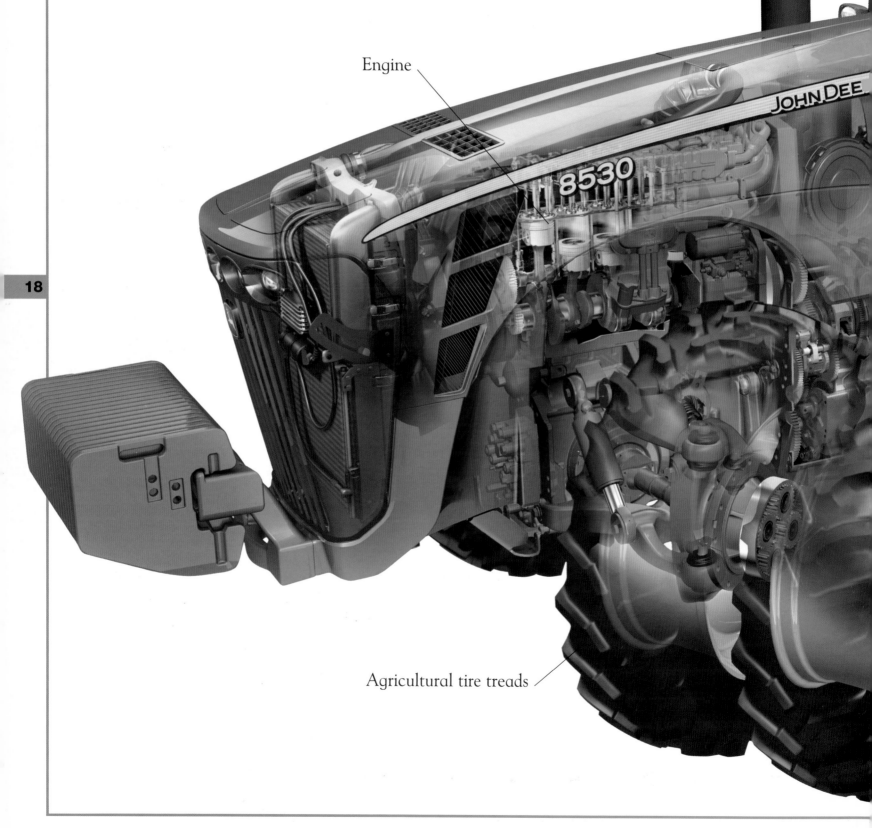

GPS receiver

Rearview and side mirrors

GPS monitor

Exhaust pipe

Engine

JOHN DEE

8530

Agricultural tire treads

Back window

Cab

Turn signals

Wheel rims

Steps

Axle

◄ Now look inside to see how a tractor is made!

From then to now

The tractor has changed a lot since it was first invented. A tractor today is bigger, heavier, and can do many more jobs than the very first tractors. Here's how it all got started for John Deere.

1911 Waterloo Boy: The Waterloo Gasoline Traction Engine Company created a gasoline-powered tractor called the Waterloo Boy. Deere & Company bought the Waterloo Company in 1918. The Waterloo Boy became the first John Deere tractor. It had 12 horsepower.

1935 Model B: This was a row-crop tractor for smaller farms or gardens. It was smaller, lighter, and used less fuel than the Model A.

1923 Model D: This was the first production tractor to have the John Deere name. It was designed for pulling plows and other implements.

1934 Model A: This tractor was built for crops planted in rows. It had rear wheels that could be adjusted to fit between rows of different sizes.

1947 Model M: This tractor came with an easier way for farmers to attach and control implements.

1924 Model DI: This was the first tractor built for industrial jobs. It was also the first yellow John Deere tractor. Now all John Deere construction machines are yellow.

1928 Model GP: "GP" stands for *general purpose*—which means this tractor could do many different jobs, such as operate a thresher, pull a mower, or pull a plow or seeder.

J.T.'s TRACTOR TRIVIA

Do you know what a Johnny Popper is? It is the name that people called the first John Deere tractors, because when they drove they made a pop-pop sound.

1973 Model 4630: This tractor was the first to have sound protection in the cab. The cab was also designed to protect farmers if the tractor rolled over.

1969 Model 4520: This tractor had the first turbocharged engine. This means that the engine used more fuel and air to give the tractor extra power.

1983 Model 4050: This tractor could turn more sharply than any tractor before, and could drive at 15 different speeds. It was also the quietest tractor at this time.

1964 Model 4020: This was the most popular tractor in the 1960s because it was available for six different kinds of farming.

2006 Model 9620: This is the biggest and most powerful John Deere tractor to date. It has up to 500 horsepower and can have up to 12 wheels.

25

Tractors on the farm

There are many different kinds of farms, and the tractor is the most important machine on most of them. Farmers on small farms have tough little tractors. Farmers with large farms have giant tractors that can drive across huge fields and pull very heavy loads. Look how many different kinds of jobs tractors do on farms.

Plowing fields

Packing big bundles

Harvesting crops

Lifting big loads

Mowing grass

Mulching soil

Hauling heavy cargo

Plow!

Over the winter, the ground gets hard, and farmers need to loosen it before they can plant their crops. One of the tractor's main jobs is to loosen the soil. This is called plowing, or tilling, the fields. Farmers till their fields in the spring. They attach plows to their tractors. The plow breaks up the hard ground so that air and water can reach a plant's roots more easily.

The three-point hitch is where the plow and other implements are attached.

JOHN DEERE

Shares, which are curved blades, go into the area cut by the coulters and dig even deeper. They create furrows, which are straight rows or grooves across the field.

Coulters are sharp, steel blades. They cut straight into the soil first.

Grow!

After tilling, the soil is ready. Now it's time to plant the seeds. Before there were tractors, farmers would walk up and down acres and acres of fields and plant the seeds by hand. This took a long time! With a tractor, farmers can seed an area equal to 100 football fields in just one day.

Air drill

Different kinds of implements plant different kinds of crops, but an air drill is the most common kind. It plants small grains, such as wheat, barley, and oats. A tractor pulls the air drill, which makes holes in the furrows. All the holes have the same amount of space between them. Then the drill drops seeds into them.

The closing wheel rolls behind the press wheel. It covers the seeds with soil.

The hopper holds the seeds. There is a small opening at the bottom so the seeds can drop through the machine into the soil.

The press wheel pushes the seeds down to the bottom of the furrow, where they will grow best.

Other kinds of crops

There are many different kinds of seeds, so there are also many different kinds of implements. Here are other implements that tractors pull to plant crops.

A box drill is a lot like the air drill, but it can also be used for bigger seeds, such as soybeans.

Soybean field

Integral planters are used for bigger plants, like corn, beans, sugar beets, cotton, and peanuts. Planters are also used for seedlings. The planter scoops out a small hole, drops the seedling in, and then covers the hole with dirt.

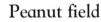

Peanut field

Fold and go

The drill is very wide, so it can plant seeds in many rows at the same time. When a farmer drives the drill from one field to another, or back to the storage shed, the drill folds up so it doesn't bump into anything along the way.

Spread and spray

Once the seeds begin to grow, farmers must care for the crops and protect them. Farmers have to make sure their crops get the right amount of sunlight and water, and they protect them from weeds. Weeds are unwanted plants that use the food and water meant for the crops. There are a few different ways tractors help farmers keep their crops healthy.

Cultivators

A cultivator is an implement that combs the soil between the rows of plants. The cultivator has teeth like a rake that pull up weeds between the plants.

Sprayers

Some farmers use sprayer implements to spray weeds with liquid herbicides. Herbicides are chemicals that destroy the weeds but not the crops.

Tractors have special sprayers for orchard trees.

J.T.'s TRACTOR TRIVIA

Farmers do not spray pesticides on windy days. They don't want the wind to carry the pesticides to other areas.

Don't bug me!

Bugs, worms, and other pests may eat and destroy crops. Some of the "baddest bugs" on a farm are aphids, caterpillars, boll weevils, and beetles. Sprayers can also be used to cover crops with pesticides, which destroy these unwanted bugs.

Caterpillar

Special jobs

Tractors of all sizes are important on farms, especially during harvest season. Sometimes tractors help other machines harvest the crops and haul the heavy loads. Let's take a look at different ways tractors help.

Wheat and corn harvesting

During the summer, wheat and corn grow big and tall. In the fall, it's time to harvest. Tractors work together with machines called combines to collect the grain from plants. As the combine separates the grain from the plant stalks, the tractor drives alongside it to collect the grain in big wagons. The two machines have to drive at exactly the same speed.

Spout

Combine

Gravity bin

Potato and sugar beet harvesting

Tractors also pull special implements to harvest vegetables that grow under the ground, such as potatoes and sugar beets. This implement scoops plants out of the ground, cuts off the stems, and drops the vegetables into a truck's collection bin.

Potato harvesting

Sugar beet harvesting

Cotton harvesting

Special machines called cotton pickers harvest the cotton, but tractors pull implements like this one to pick up any leftover cotton and pack it into big bundles.

Bale, lift, and load

In the summer, farmers cut tall grasses, called forage, and leave it in the field to dry in the sun. After the dried grass turns yellow or brown, it's called hay. Hay is used to feed the animals in the winter. But loose hay is hard to move, so before moving hay from a field to the barn, it is first made into hay bales.

Baler

Bale chamber

Suitcase weights

Baling Hay

1. Balers are machines that tractors pull over the fields to suck up the loose hay.
2. The hay goes into the bale chamber where rubber rollers spin the hay around tightly to make the bale.
3. Inside the baler, twine or plastic is wrapped around the bale to hold it together.
4. Finally, the baler opens and drops the bale onto the field to dry some more.

Lifting and loading

After the hay is rolled into bales, it needs to be moved to a barn or another field. But hay bales are heavy. Usually a bale spike is attached to the front of the tractor. The point is poked into the center of a hay bale to lift it. Some farmers add a pallet fork to the front of their tractors, which turns the tractor into a forklift.

J.T.'s TRACTOR TRIVIA

A handful of hay might be very light, but balers pick up so much hay that just one round hay bale can weigh up to 2,000 pounds—that's the same as a small car.

What are suitcase weights?

Suitcase weights are special weights added to the front or back of a tractor for balance. They help keep a tractor steady and evenly weighted when it is pulling or lifting very heavy loads. They are called suitcase weights because they look a little bit like suitcases.

All in a row

Farmers use different kinds of tractors for different crops. Think about apples and lettuce. Apples grow on trees. Lettuce grows low to the ground. The same kind of tractor can't take care of these different kinds of crops. Let's take a look at some different tractors for different crops.

Hi-Crop tractors

Some crops, such as lettuce, soybeans, peanuts, and watermelons grow in rows called beds. The beds are low to the ground. They can grow up to two feet tall. A Hi-Crop tractor's wheels fit in between the rows and its underside is higher, so it doesn't crush the plants.

Narrow tractors

Cherry trees grow in orchards and grapes grow in vineyards. Orchards and vineyards have long rows of trees and vines with only a few feet of space between each row. Tractors must be able to drive through the rows of trees to spray them for pests, pick the weeds, and mow the grass. There's a special tractor for orchards and vineyards called a Narrow Crop Tractor or Orchard Tractor. It is much narrower than other farm tractors, but it still has the same amount of power.

A shorter cab height lets the tractor pass without hitting tall vines.

The narrow chassis lets the tractor fit in tight spaces.

A really big tractor

The bigger the tractor is, the more work it can do.
Some tractors are so big that they need 8, 10, or even 12
tires. Here's a really big tractor!

J.T.'s TRACTOR TRIVIA

This tractor's fuel tank is so big that it
holds 180 gallons of fuel. That's 20 times
more fuel than an average car holds!

Tractor stats

Weight: 25,000 pounds
Horsepower: 250 hp
Number of wheels: 8
Tire height: 81 inches—that's 7 feet, 9 inches tall. How tall are you? Not as tall as these tires!
Number of speeds: 18 different forward speeds and 6 reverse speeds

Compact utility tractors

Compact utility tractors are smaller, narrower, and have less horsepower than big farm tractors. But they can still do most of the same jobs. These tractors are often used on small farms, where farmers have less room between crops and need smaller implements.

The steering wheel and onboard computer work the same way as the ones in big tractors.

Under the hood, there is a small diesel engine. Most compact utility tractors have between 40 and 60 horsepower.

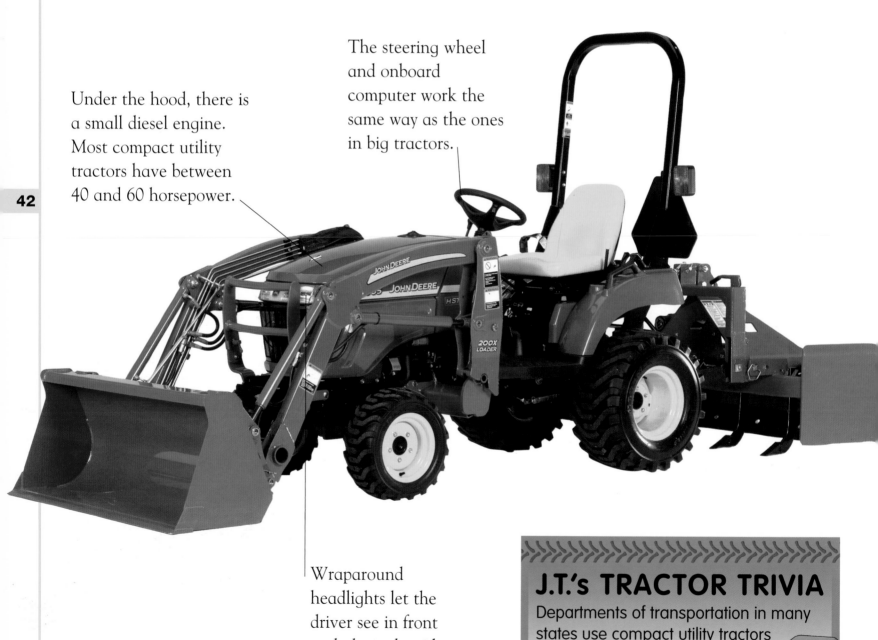

Wraparound headlights let the driver see in front and along the sides at night.

J.T.'s TRACTOR TRIVIA

Departments of transportation in many states use compact utility tractors to mow the grass alongside highways and interstates.

Scoop!

Loader buckets attach to the front of a compact utility tractor. A loader is like a huge shovel. It can scoop up things such as dirt, gravel, and wood chips.

Lift!

Pallet forks also attach to the front of a compact utility tractor to help lift and carry heavy items. This tractor is moving potted plants.

Move!

Compact utility tractors can also help move heavy objects around the farm or yard. This loader bucket is being filled with firewood.

Lawn tractors

Years ago, if you wanted to cut your grass, the only choice you had was to stand behind a heavy mower and push. This was a lot of work, especially for really big lawns. Now, people can sit comfortably as they drive a small tractor to cut their lawn.

Small but tough

Lawn tractors are the smallest type of tractor, but they are still tough. They usually have a 15 to 25 horsepower engine. They are mostly used for mowing lawns but can also be used for driving over rough, bumpy ground.

Lawn tractors have a speed control lever just like big tractors.

Lawn tractors have sharp, scissorlike blades to trim the grass. This safety cover protects the driver from the spinning blades.

After being cut, the grass clippings come out of this chute.

Multipurpose machines

Lawn tractors aren't just for mowing grass. They can:

- haul shrubs that need to be planted
- spread fertilizer or grass seed on a lawn
- till the garden
- pick up or blow leaves
- load dirt, mulch, or gravel

Headlights are useful for mowing at dusk.

J.T.'s TRACTOR TRIVIA

Some lawn tractors have regular steering wheels to turn. But others have two handles, one for each hand. The driver changes direction just by moving one handle—his left hand to go left and his right hand to go right.

These tires have turf treads, which don't damage the grass as the tractor drives over it.

Tractors in the winter

In the spring, summer, and fall, the tractor plants, mows, and harvests. What does a tractor do in the winter? Let's see.

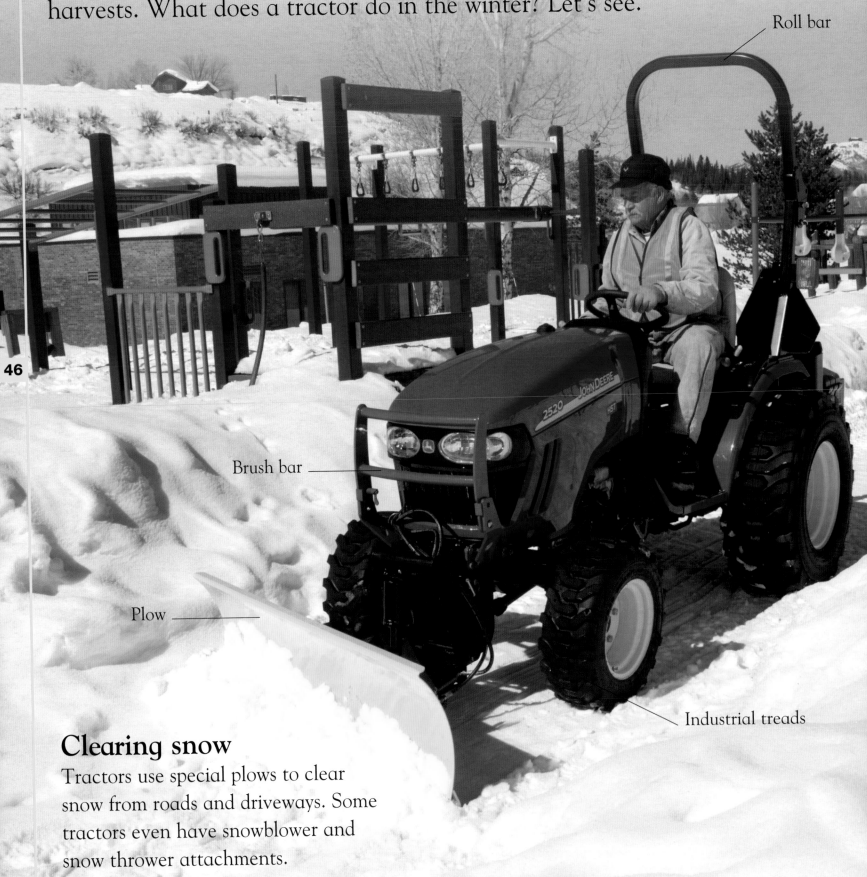

Roll bar

Brush bar

Plow

Industrial treads

Clearing snow

Tractors use special plows to clear snow from roads and driveways. Some tractors even have snowblower and snow thrower attachments.

Winter feedings

In the winter, farmers use their tractors to haul grain and hay bales from the silo to feed their animals.

47

Icy ground

Tractors have better traction than cars on ice—they can drive over surfaces that would make a car slip and slide. But when the ground is really slippery, even tractors might slide on the ice. Tractor tires can be wrapped in chains, so they don't slide.

Christmas!

Christmas tree farms use tractors. This one is taking people on a hayride to cut down their own trees.

Making old tractors new

Many people enjoy restoring tractors. Tractor restoration means taking an old tractor and fixing it up so it runs and looks the way it did when it first left the factory many years ago. And when you restore a tractor, you learn how a tractor works—from the inside out.

Tractor restoration for kids

You don't have to wait until you are a grown-up to restore a tractor! Many high schools have FFA (agricultural science education) groups or Agricultural Mechanics classes that teach tractor restoration. In fact, every year there is a big competition called the Chevron Delo Tractor Restoration Competition. In this competition, high-school-age FFA members, either alone or in groups, compete to see who can restore an antique tractor the best.

Before

After

Shane Blaes won first prize for restoring this 1944 tractor. Now it drives like new.

J.T.'s TRACTOR TRIVIA

You can find out what year a tractor was made by looking at the serial number on the right side of the tractor.

After

Before

Eighteen-year-old Tyler Raska worked very hard to make his grandfather's tractor look brand-new again. Tyler's younger sister restores tractors, too, and they always help each other out.

After

When she was 15 years old, Tabetha Salsbury found this tractor that had been sitting in a field for over 30 years and completely restored it. Tabatha has been helping her father and grandfather fix tractors since she was six years old!

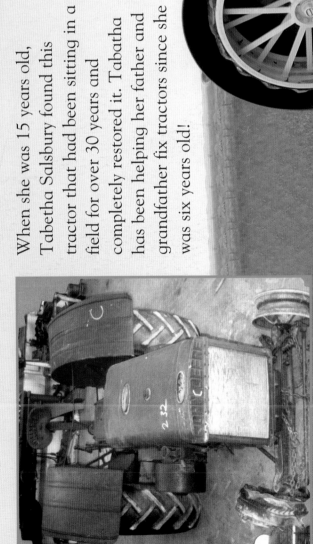

Before

Tractor fun

We know that tractors are used for hard work. But ask any farmer, and he or she will tell you that tractors are a lot of fun, too. Tractors can take kids on hayrides, drive people out to the fields for a fun day of apple picking, and even line up for a parade through town.

Pumpkin picking

Pumpkins are grown in pumpkin patches. The full-grown pumpkins need to be picked by hand, and the tractor drives the pumpkin pickers to the field.

The world's largest pumpkin, grown in 2006, weighed in at 1,502 pounds. You definitely need a tractor to move a pumpkin this heavy.

50

Everyone loves a parade!

Big tractors, small tractors, old tractors, and new tractors all make their way down Main Street for a tractor parade. Some tractor parades are held at night, and the tractors are decorated with tiny lights.

Tractor safety

The tractor is often called the farmer's best friend. But tractors can be extremely dangerous, too. It's important to know how to be safe around these powerful machines. Here are some important rules for tractor safety.

It's a machine, not a ride

Tractors are made for one adult to drive and operate—not for kids. No one should ever ride on any outside part of the tractor, such as the fender, the bucket, or the axle. Most accidents happen when extra riders fall off moving tractors. The rule is always: one seat, one rider.

Inside the cab

Some tractors have enclosed cabs, and some have open ones, but both of them have important features to keep the driver safe. The most important is the Rollover Protection System (ROPS), which is a bar that stops the driver from being crushed if the tractor rolls over. But it's also important that every driver wear the seat belt at all times.

Stay in clear sight

No one should stand anywhere near a tractor. The driver must be able to see other people at all times. Don't run alongside the machine—the driver might turn and not know you are there. Never stand behind a tractor or farm machine.

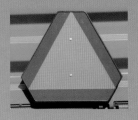

On the roads

When tractors drive on roads, they need Slow Moving Vehicle stickers. This sticker shows cars that the tractor can go only as fast as 25 miles per hour. On many roads cars can drive twice as fast as that. The SMV sticker is triangle-shaped and is bright orange bordered in red. See if you can spot one the next time you see a tractor.

Lawn tractors are tractors!

Even though they are smaller than most tractors, lawn tractors are powerful machines that are meant for only one adult to operate. Lawn tractors have very sharp, spinning blades for mowing grass that can seriously hurt you if your hand or foot gets too close to them.

Danger! High voltage!

Always stay away from the Power Take-Off bar. The PTO has a lot of power and is very dangerous if touched. Because this bar spins so fast, loose clothing and hair can easily get caught. Also, even if a tractor is turned off, it's still not safe to touch. Parts of the tractor get very hot. And if a control is touched, the tractor could move backward or forward.

Eyes wide open

Always remember that a tractor is a powerful machine and not a toy. The most important rule is: never be near a tractor alone. Always have an adult with you. Stay alert, and be safe!

One machine for every job

If you have a tractor, you can do almost anything!

Lift heavy loads of gravel

Till the soil

Move lots of dirt

Landscape golf courses

Haul fertilizer

Dump big loads

Take a kid-sized ride!

Glossary

Agricultural tires
Tires with treads in diagonal lines, so soil doesn't stick to them.

Air drill
A planting attachment used for small grains like wheat, barley, and oats.

Axle
The rod that connects the wheels to the tractor and to each other.

Bale spike
An attachment that allows tractors to move big bales of hay.

Baler
An attachment that collects loose hay from the field and rolls it into hay bales.

Box drill
A planting implement used for bigger seeds like soybeans.

Chassis
The metal body of the tractor.

Combination tires
Tires with treads that get good traction on fields but can also be used on turf.

Combine
A special machine used to harvest grains, such as wheat and corn.

Cultivator
An implement that combs the soil to pull up weeds between the plants.

Cylinder
The part of an engine where fuel is burned.

Forage
Tall grasses that are cut and made into hay bales.

Front rib tires
Tires used on the front wheels of smaller tractors.

Herbicide
A chemical that destroys unwanted weeds but not crops.

Horsepower
The amount of pulling power an engine has.

Implements
The tractor's important attachments, like plows and planters.

Integral planter
A planting implement used for bigger plants and seedlings.

Pallet fork
An attachment that turns the tractor into a forklift to move heavy objects.

Pesticide
A chemical that destroys unwanted bugs that can harm crops.

Power Take-Off system (PTO)
A metal pole that sends power from the tractor's engine to the implements.

Tilling
Preparing the soil for planting by breaking up and loosening the soil.

Transmission
The part of the engine that controls the gears, which control the tractor's speed.

Turf tires
Tires that don't damage grass, and are usually found on lawn tractors.

56

Picture credits

The publisher would like to thank the following for their kind permission to reproduce their photographs:

ABBREVIATIONS KEY:
t-top, b-bottom, r-right, l-left, c-center

6-7: Deborah Hewitt/Dreamstime.com (7tr);
10-11: John Vachon/USDA (11tr);
16-17: Vladimir Mucibabik/ Shutterstock, Inc. (16bl); Rod Beverley/Shutterstock, Inc. (16br); Marek Pawluczuk/Shutterstock, Inc. (17bl);
20-23: Greg McCracken/ Shutterstock, Inc. (21cr);
30-31: Clayton Thacker/Shutterstock, Inc (31cl); Joe Gough/Shutterstock, Inc. (31cr);
32-33: Sascha Burkard/Shutterstock, Inc. (32c); New York Apple Association (33t); Michael Ledray/Shutterstock, Inc. (33br);
46-47: Photodisc/Punchstock.com (47bl); Elena Elisseeva/Big Stock Photo (47br);
48-49: Photos courtesy of Shane Blaes (48tr/48br); Photos courtesy of Tyler Raska (49tl/49tr); Photos courtesy of Tabetha Salsbury (49bl/49br);
50-51: Phil Leckrone/Stuckmeyers, Inc. Fenton, MO (50br); Copyright Matt Knowles (51t); Rick Sargeant/Big Stock Photo (51c); Aaron Whitney/Big Stock Photo (51b);
52-53: Andreas Gradin/Shutterstock, Inc. (52t); Joseph Helfenberger/ Dreamstime.com (52c); Marek Pawluczuk/Shutterstock, Inc. (53t); Kris Butler/Shutterstock, Inc. (53c); Denise Beverly/Dreamstime.com (53b);
54-55: Peg Perego (55br);
All other images © Deere & Company.